A Spirituality of Fundraising

Henri J. M. Nouwen

John S. Mogabgab, *Series Editor*

UPPER
ROOM BOOKS®

NASHVILLE

The Upper Room Web site: www.upperroom.org
Henri Nouwen Society website: www.HenriNouwen.org

This material was originally co-published with the Henri Nouwen Society in 2004 in booklet form.

UPPER ROOM®, UPPER ROOM BOOKS®, and design logos are trade-
marks owned by The Upper Room®, a ministry of GBOD®, Nashville, Ten-
nessee. All rights reserved.

Unless otherwise indicated, Scripture quotations are from the New Re-
vised Standard Version Bible, copyright © 1989, Division of Christian
Education of the National Council of Churches of Christ in the United
States of America. Used by permission. All rights reserved.

Scripture quotations designated NJB are taken from The New Jerusalem
Bible, copyright © 1985 by Darton, Longman & Todd, Ltd. and Double-
day, a division of Random House, Inc. Reprinted by permission.

Cover and Interior Design: Sue Smith and Pearson & Co.
Cover art: Gogh, Vincent van, (1888). The Sower. Erich Lessing / Art
Resource, NY
Photo on page 62 by Mary Ellen Kronstein. Used by permission.

Library of Congress Cataloging-in-Publication Data
Nouwen, Henri J. M.
A spirituality of fundraising / by Henri J. M. Nouwen.
p. cm. — (The Henri Nouwen spirituality series)
"List of Henri Nouwen's works cited"— P.
ISBN 978-0-8358-1044-9
I. Church fundraising. I. Title.
BV772.5.N68 2011
 254'.8—dc22

                                                        2010040997

Printed in the United States of America

CONTENTS

About the Henri Nouwen Spirituality Series   *iv*

Preface   *v*

Acknowledgments   *x*

Fundraising as Ministry   15

Helping the Kingdom Come About   23

Our Security Base   26

People Who Are Rich   34

Asking   42

A New Communion   47

Prayer and Gratitude   54

Your Kingdom Come   59

Henri J. M. Nouwen's Works Cited   61

About Henri J. M. Nouwen   62

ABOUT THE HENRI NOUWEN SPIRITUALITY SERIES

H ENRI NOUWEN sought the center of things. Never content to observe life from the sidelines, his approach to new experiences and relationships was full throttle. He looked at the world with the enthusiastic anticipation of a child, convinced that right in the midst of life he would find the God who loves us without conditions. Helping us recognize this God in the very fabric of our lives was the enduring passion of Henri's life and ministry.

The Henri Nouwen Spirituality Series embodies Henri's legacy of compassionate engagement with contemporary issues and concerns. Developed through a partnership between the Henri Nouwen Society and Upper Room Ministries, the Series offers fresh presentations of themes close to Henri's heart. We hope each volume will help you discover that in your daily round God is closer than you think.

PREFACE

S PEAKING ONE DAY to a large audience gathered to hear about fundraising as ministry, Henri Nouwen learned that the booksellers in the lobby had sold all their copies of his latest book. At noon, he set out for the nearest bookstore to purchase more copies for them to have on hand. En route to his car, he was approached by a casually dressed young man who requested money to get home in France. Characteristically, Henri said, "Jump into the car and come with me. Tell me about yourself."

As they drove along, the young man explained his unsuccessful attempt to secure a hoped-for position in Canada and his inability to get to his home because of lack of funds. Return ticket in hand, he was leaving that evening for Paris but had no money to get from there to his hometown in the south of France. When Henri had completed his purchase, returned to the conference center, and as they were parting,

Henri gave the young man two hundred dollars and asked him to send news upon his safe arrival home.

Later that day, following his lectures and just before leaving, the booksellers in the lobby handed Henri an envelope in gratitude for his kindness to them. Opening the card, Henri found a thank-you note and a check for two hundred dollars!

Generosity begets generosity. This is especially so when generosity is rooted in the rich soil of relatedness. Henri, because of his open and Spirit-filled attitude, always sought points of relatedness with the people he met. Henri's generosity with money grew from a larger generosity of self. His desire for authentic relationships stirred this desire in others, and so he experienced people as generous with their time, their concern, and also their money.

In many ways, Henri was a rich and generous man with the means and the openness to give. He also needed funds to support his many passionate interests. So he experienced fundraising from both sides, and his vision of it arose from his actual experience of being asked to donate money and of asking others to support his various ministries. Then, with time, his vision extended beyond the personal to the universal.

Like many of us, Henri's vision began with the notion of fundraising "as a necessary but unpleasant activity to support spiritual things." But his passion for ministry and for living from a spiritual motivation led him further and deeper until he could finally say with conviction, "Fundraising is first and foremost a form of ministry."

In this short talk Henri is on fire and passionate about God's kingdom. He offers all those motivated by the Spirit of God a new set of glasses to see and live their fundraising ministry as integral to their mission: "Fundraising is as spiritual as giving a sermon, entering a time of prayer, visiting the sick, or feeding the hungry!"

As ministry, fundraising includes proclamation and invitation as well as conversion.

"Fundraising is proclaiming what we believe in such a way that we offer other people an opportunity to participate with us in our vision and mission." For Henri, the proclamation and invitation involve a challenging call to conversion for fund-raisers and donors alike. "Fundraising is always a call to conversion." All are called into a new, more spiritual relationship with their needs and their resources. Henri encourages fundraisers to become more confident and joyful, standing up in their asking without apology. And in this vision they do not profit alone, because donors also participate in a new communion with others while becoming part of a much larger spiritual vision and fruitfulness.

Because of the fruitful relationship between the Henri Nouwen Society and Upper Room Ministries, this project and its passage from idea to reality authenticate the manuscript's spiritual message about ministry, vision, asking, giving, and receiving. I believe and trust that the collective investment of so many people in creating this book will be multiplied many times through its impact on the fundraising vision and practice of countless individuals and organizations.

Sue Mosteller, CSJ
The Henri Nouwen Legacy Trust

ACKNOWLEDGMENTS

O N September 16, 1992, Henri Nouwen spoke to the Marguerite Bourgeoys Family Service Foundation about fundraising. It was an informal address that came from the heart without need of a written manuscript. Happily, the talk was recorded on tape and the transcript lightly edited. From time to time copies of the talk were given to individuals or organizations involved in fundraising ventures. The positive response to the fresh vision of fundraising that Henri was beginning to articulate led Sue Mosteller, Henri's literary executrix, to consider ways of distributing the piece more widely.

The manuscript was given as a gift to the fledgling Henri Nouwen Society for its own work in financial development. In April 2003, I was contacted about the possibility of preparing Henri's text for publication. The call from the Nouwen Society was inspired by my relationship with Henri. During my doctoral studies at Yale

University I served for five years as Henri's teaching, research, and editorial assistant. He was my mentor and friend. *Weavings*, the journal I edited for twenty-four years, still seeks to reflect in its own time and place the spiritual vision that Henri so beautifully embodied.

I have exercised the liberty that Henri regularly granted me to add material where his ideas invited expansion or his transitions needed elaboration. Labors of love attract community, and this project has confirmed that truth. Nathan Ball and Sue Mosteller from the Nouwen Legacy Trust have been deeply involved in all aspects of the work. Despite a ferocious schedule, Sue even found time to write the Preface. Wendy Greer and Robert Durback generously offered suggestions for the margin excerpts from Henri's other writings. Resa Pearson, Elaine Go, and Sue Smith of Pearson & Company created a design as appealing and accessible as Henri's life and faith. Pamela Hawkins reviewed the manuscript with an editor's careful eye. And Robin Pippin of

Upper Room Books guided the whole process with gentle skill. Finally, I would like to thank you, the reader, for taking up Henri's vision of fundraising as ministry and carrying it forward in ways he could hardly have imagined.

John S. Mogabgab
Upper Room Ministries

Make love your aim.

(1 Corinthians 14:1, NJB)

FUNDRAISING IS a subject we seldom think about from a spiritual perspective. We may think of fundraising as a necessary but unpleasant activity to support spiritual things. Or we might believe that fundraising reflects a failure to plan well or to trust enough that God will provide for all our needs. Indeed, quite often fundraising is a response to a crisis. Suddenly our organization or faith community does not have enough money, so we begin to say: "How are we going to get the money we need? We have to start asking for it." Then we realize that we are not used to doing this. We may feel awkward and a little embarrassed about it. We begin to worry and wonder: "Who will give us money? How will we ask them?"

Fundraising
as Ministry

Ministry is, first of all, receiving God's blessing from those to whom we minister. What is this blessing? It is a glimpse of the face of God.

—Here and Now

FUNDRAISING AS MINISTRY

From the perspective of the gospel, fundraising is not a response to a crisis. Fundraising is, first and foremost, a form of ministry. It is a way of announcing our vision and inviting other people into our mission. Vision and mission are so central to the life of God's people that without vision we perish and without mission we lose our way (Prov. 29:18; 2 Kings 21:1-9). Vision brings together needs and resources to meet those needs (Acts 9:1-19). Vision also shows us new directions and opportunities for our mission (Acts 16:9-10). Vision gives us courage to speak when we might want to remain silent (Acts 18:9).

Fundraising is proclaiming what we believe in such a way that we offer other people an opportunity to participate with us in our vision and mission. Fundraising is precisely the opposite of begging. When we seek to raise funds we are not saying, "Please, could you help us out because lately it's been hard." Rather, we are declaring, "We have a vision that is amazing and exciting. We are inviting you to invest yourself through the resources that God has given you—your energy, your prayers, and your money—in this work to which God has called us." Our invitation is clear and confident because we trust that our vision and mission are like "trees planted by streams of water, which yield their fruit in its season, and their leaves do not wither" (Ps. 1:3).

Fundraising is also always a call to conversion. And this call comes to both those who seek funds and those who have funds. Whether we are asking for money or giving money we are drawn together by God, who is about to do a new thing through our collaboration (see Isa. 43:19). To be converted means to experience a deep shift in how we see and

Indeed, living a spiritual life requires a change of heart, a conversion. Such a conversion may be marked by a sudden inner change, or it can take place through a long, quiet process of transformation.

—Making All Things New

think and act. To be converted is to be clothed in our right mind, to come to ourselves the way the younger son did when he was starving far from his true home (Luke 15:14-20). It is a shift of attention in which we set our mind on divine things (Matt. 16:23). "Do not be conformed to this world, but be transformed by the renewing of your minds, so that you may discern what is the will of God—what is good and acceptable and perfect" (Rom. 12:2). Fundraising as ministry involves a real conversion.

In fundraising, people who work in the marketplace are often wiser than people who work in the church. Those who are involved in big business know that you never get much money if you beg for it. I remember visiting a successful fundraiser in Texas whose office was filled with beautiful things. I said, "How do you dare to ask for money in this office?" He replied, "My office is part of my way of approaching people. It is meant to communicate that I know how to work with money, that I know how to make money grow. This inspires confidence in the people I meet that their investment will be well used."

This approach is not for everyone, and being surrounded by nice things is not the right motivation for fundraising as ministry. Important here is that spiritually this man was saying, "I ask for money standing up, not bowing down, because I believe in what I am about. I believe that I have something important to offer." Without apology he invites people to be a part of his vision.

In fundraising as ministry, we are inviting people into a new way of relating to their resources. By giving people a spiritual vision, we want them to experience that they will in fact benefit by making their resources available to us. We truly believe that if their gift is good only for us who receive, it is not fundraising in the spiritual sense. Fundraising from

The converted person sees, hears, and understands with a divine eye, a divine ear, a divine heart.

—¡Gracias!

the point of view of the gospel says to people: "I will take your money and invest it in this vision only if it is good for your spiritual journey, only if it is good for your spiritual health." In other words, we are calling them to an experience of conversion: "You won't become poorer, you will become richer by giving." We can confidently declare with the Apostle Paul: "You will be enriched in every way for your great generosity" (2 Cor. 9:11).

If this confident approach and invitation are lacking, then we are disconnected from our vision and have lost the direction of our mission. We also will be cut off from our donors, because we will find ourselves begging for money and they will find themselves merely handing us a check. No real connection has been created because we have not asked them to come and be with us. We have not given them an opportunity to participate in the spirit of what we are about. We may have completed a successful transaction, but we have not initiated a successful relationship.

Here we see that if fundraising as ministry invites those with money to a new relationship with their wealth, it also calls us to be converted in relation to our needs. If we come back from asking someone for money and we feel exhausted and somehow tainted by unspiritual activity, there is something wrong. We must not let ourselves be tricked into thinking that fundraising is only a secular activity. As a form of ministry, fundraising

God will make our love fruitful, whether we see that fruitfulness or not.
—Bread for the Journey

is as spiritual as giving a sermon, entering a time of prayer, visiting the sick, or feeding the hungry. So fundraising has to help us with our conversion too. Are we willing to be converted from our fear of asking, our anxiety about being rejected or feeling humiliated, our depression when someone says, "No, I'm not going to get involved in your project"? When we have gained the freedom to ask without fear, to love fundraising as a form of ministry, then fundraising will be good for our spiritual life.

When those with money and those who need money share a mission, we see a central sign of new life in the Spirit of Christ. We belong together in our work because Jesus has brought us together, and our fruitfulness depends on staying connected with him. Jesus tells us: "I am the vine, you are the branches. Those who abide in me and I in them bear much fruit, because apart from me you can do nothing" (John 15:5). With him, we can do anything because we know that God surrounds us with an abundance of blessings. Therefore, those who need money and those who can give money meet on the common ground of God's love. "God is able to provide you with every blessing in abundance, so that by always having enough of everything, you may share abundantly in every good work" (2 Cor. 9:8). When this happens, we can indeed say with Paul, "There is a new creation!" (2 Cor. 5:17). Where there is a new creation in Christ, there the kingdom of God is made manifest to the world.

Helping the Kingdom Come About

To set our hearts on the kingdom therefore means to make the life of the Spirit within and among us the center of all we think, say, or do.

—Making All Things New

HELPING THE KINGDOM COME ABOUT

F UNDRAISING IS A VERY concrete way to help the kingdom of God come about. What is the kingdom? Jesus is clear that if we make the kingdom our first priority, "all these other things will be given you as well" (Matt. 6:33, NJB). The kingdom is where God provides for all that we need. It is the realm of sufficiency where we are no longer pulled here and there by anxiety about having enough. "So do not worry about tomorrow: tomorrow will take care of itself" (Matt. 6:34, NJB). Jesus also compares the kingdom to a mustard seed, "which, at the time of its sowing, is the smallest of all the seeds on earth. Yet once it is sown it grows into the biggest shrub of them all and puts out big branches so that the birds of the air can shelter in its shade" (Mark 4:31-32, NJB). Even a seemingly small act of generosity can grow into something far beyond what we could ever ask or imagine (see Eph. 3:20)—the creation of a community of love in this world, and beyond this world, because wherever love grows, it is stronger than death (1 Cor. 13:8). So when we give ourselves to planting and nurturing love here on earth, our efforts will reach out beyond our own chronological existence. Indeed, if we raise funds for the creation of a community of love, we are helping God build the kingdom. We are doing exactly what we are supposed to do as Christians. Paul is clear about this: "Make love your aim" (1 Cor. 14:1, NJB).

Our Security Base

The converted person
knows himself or herself and
all the world in God.

–¡Gracias!

OUR SECURITY BASE

THOSE OF US WHO ASK for money need to look carefully at ourselves. The question is not how to get money. Rather, the question is about our relationship with money. We will never be able to ask for money if we do not know how we ourselves relate to money.

What is the place of money in our lives? The importance of money is so tied up with relationships that it seems almost impossible to think about it without also thinking about how family life has influenced our relationship with money.

How many of us know how much money our father or mother earns, or has, at the moment? Do we normally talk with them about their money? Is money ever the subject of dinner table conversation? Are family conversations about money usually anxious, angry, hopeful, satisfied? Did our parents talk with us about money when we were children? Do they talk with us about it now? Did they teach us skills in how to handle money? And in our own turn, do we discuss our financial affairs with our children? Are we comfortable telling them how we earn it and how we use it?

Money is a central reality of family relationships. It is also a central reality in our relationships with people, institutions, and causes beyond family life. Therefore we need also to think about this side of our financial life.

How do we spend the money we have? Are we inclined to save it so we will be prepared for emergencies, or do we spend it because we might not have it later? Do we like to give our money to friends, to charities, to churches, to political parties, to educational institutions? Where are we, in fact, giving our money? Are we concerned about whether our gift is tax deductible? Does that question even occur to us?

How would we feel if people used the money we gave them in ways other than those for which we gave it? Imagine giving a thousand dollars to someone thinking the money would be used to help needy children. Later it becomes clear that this person used the donation for a trip to the Caribbean. Would we get angry? Once a seminary president said to me, "If you never want to be fooled, you will never give money."

If money touches our relationships with family members as well as the world beyond our home, it also reaches into our inner life. It is interesting that the phrase "personal worth" can mean both the extent of our financial assets and our value as a human being. Once again, some questions may help us explore this aspect of our relationship with money.

How does having, or not having, money affect our self-esteem, our sense of value? Do we feel good about ourselves when we have a lot of money? If we do not have much money, do we feel bad about ourselves? Is a low or even modest income a source of embarrassment? Or do we think money doesn't matter at all?

Money and power go together. There is also a real relationship between power and a sense of self-worth. Do we ever use money to control people or events? In other words, do we use our money to make things happen the way we want them to happen? Do we ever use money simply to give others the freedom to do what they want to do? How do we feel when people ask us for money?

If any of these questions makes us uncomfortable, it may be because talking about money is one of the greatest taboos around. Money conversations are a greater taboo than conversations about sex or religion. People may say, "Don't talk about religion, that's my private business." Others may say, "Don't talk about sex, it belongs in the bedroom." Discussing money is even harder for many people. And this becomes immediately noticeable when we must do some fundraising. Often we do not feel that asking for money is an easy thing to be "up front" about.

The reason for the taboo is that money has something to do with that intimate place in our heart where we need security, and we do not want to reveal our need or give away our security to someone who, maybe only accidentally, might betray us. Many voices around and within us warn us of the danger of dependence. We fear being dependent on others because of the idea that dependence is a threat to our security. A friend once told me how often his father would say, "Son, be sure you don't become dependent on anybody. Be sure you do not have to beg for what you need. Be sure that you always have enough money so you can have your own house, your own things, and your own people to help you. As long as you have some money in the bank, nothing bad can really happen to you."

The pressure in our culture to secure our own future and to control our lives as much

> *The Spirit of Love says: "Don't be afraid to let go of your need to control your own life.*
> —Here and Now

as possible does not find support in the Bible. Jesus knows our need for security. He is concerned that because security is such a deep human need, we do not misplace our trust in things or people that cannot offer us real security. "Do not store up treasures for yourselves on earth, where moth and woodworm destroy them and thieves can break in and steal. But store up treasures for yourselves in heaven, where neither moth nor woodworm destroys them and thieves cannot break in and steal. For wherever your treasure is, there will your heart be too" (Matt. 6:19-21, NJB). We cannot find security if our heart is divided. So Jesus says something very radical: "No servant can be the slave of two masters: he will either hate the first and love the second, or be attached to the first and despise the second. You cannot be the slave both of God and of money" (Luke 16:13, NJB).

What is our security base? God or mammon? That is what Jesus would ask. He says that we cannot put our security in God and also in money. We have to make a choice. Jesus counsels: "Put your security in God." We have to make a choice whether we want to belong to the world or to God. Our trust, our basic trust, Jesus teaches, has to be in God. As long as our real trust is in money, we cannot be true members of the kingdom. All those questions I asked were simply to help us consider whether we are, perhaps, still putting our security in money. "Those who trust in their riches will wither, but the righteous will flourish like green leaves" (Prov. 11:28). What is the true base of our security?

A truly spiritual life is life in which we won't rest until we have found rest in the embrace of the One who is the Father and Mother of all desires.

—Here and Now

People Who Are Rich

You are sent into this world
to believe in yourself as God's
chosen one and then to help
your brothers and sisters know
that they also are beloved sons
and daughters of God who
belong together.

—*Finding My Way Home*

PEOPLE WHO ARE RICH

THE BIBLE IS UNAMBIGUOUS about God's concern for the poor. "Since there will never cease to be some in need on the earth, I therefore command you, 'Open your hand to the poor and needy neighbor in your land'" (Deut. 15:11; see Isaiah 58:6–12). From its birth the church has recognized the privileged place of the poor in God's sight. "Listen, my beloved brothers and sisters. Has not God chosen the poor in the world to be rich in faith and to be heirs of the kingdom that he has promised to those who love him?" (James 2:5). Indeed, the poor and suffering remind us that the Son of God became poor for our sake (2 Cor. 8:9). God loves the poor, and so do those who follow Christ. In loving and serving the poor, we have the beautiful opportunity to love and serve Jesus. "In truth I tell you," Jesus says to his disciples, "in so far as you did this to one of the least of these brothers of mine, you did it to me" (Matt. 25:40, NJB).

But sometimes our concern for the poor may carry with it a prejudice against the rich. We may feel that they are not as good as the poor. I remember hearing a professor at a theological school say about a large, wealthy church: "This cannot be an authentic church." Perhaps we think the rich have more money than they deserve, or that they got their wealth at the expense of the poor. Maybe we find it hard to love the rich as much as the poor. But nobody says we should love the rich less than we love the poor. The poor are indeed held in the heart of God. We need to remember that the rich are held there too. I have met a number of wealthy people over the years. More and more, my experience is that rich people are also poor, but in other ways.

Many rich people are very lonely. Many struggle with a sense of being used. Others suffer from feelings of rejection or depression. It may seem strange to say, but the rich need a lot of attention and care. This is very important to recognize, because so often I have come in touch with rich people who are totally in the prison of thinking, "The only thing people see in me is money. Wherever I go, I am the rich aunt or the rich friend or the rich person, so I stay in my little circle, because as soon as I leave it people say, 'She's rich!'"

Once a woman came to see me. She was very wealthy and very depressed. She had been from one psychiatrist to another and had paid them huge fees with few results. She said, "You know, Henri, everybody is after my money. I was born into wealth and my family is wealthy. That's part of who I am, but that's not all there is. I am so afraid that I am loved only because of my money and not because of who I really am."

The roots of loneliness are very deep and cannot be touched by optimistic advertisement, substitute love images or social togetherness. They find their food in the suspicion that there is no one who cares and offers love without conditions, and no place where we can be vulnerable without being used.
—Reaching Out

Some years ago a person who had read a number of my books called my assistant at the university where I was teaching. He said, "I'm reading Henri Nouwen's books, and I wonder, does he need any money? I really want him to write more, and it is expensive to write books these days." I was away for four months, so my assistant called me and said, "There is a banker here who wants to help you with money." I did not know what to do, so I said, "Well, go and have dinner with him." So they went out for dinner and then continued to have dinner every week. They talked about all sorts of things and by the time I returned to the university, the two had become good friends.

I joined my assistant for dinner with the banker, who said, "Henri, I know you don't know a thing about money." I said, "How do you know?" He answered, "I know people like writers don't know a thing about money." What he was really saying, however, was, "What you are writing about is something I want to talk with you about on a more personal level than I can by just reading your books. I believe that the only way I can develop a personal relationship with you is through my strength, which is being a banker." Ultimately, this man was saying, "I need something that I think you have, and I really would like to get to know you." I replied, "Let's not talk about money right now. Let's just talk about you."

Over time we became close friends. Year after year he would give me a few thousand dollars. I used the money well and told him what I had done with his gift. But the money was not the most important part of our relationship. Most important was that he was able to share who he was and I was able to do the same in an atmosphere of mutual respect and trust.

When my friend died his family said to me, "We would like to continue supporting you because of the love that you had for our husband and our father. We want you always to feel that there are people who will support you because we love you, as our husband and father loved you."

Through the poverty of the rich man something very much of the kingdom developed. The money was real, but it was not the most impressive part of our relationship. We all had resources: mine were spiritual and theirs were material. What was impressive was that we all wanted to work for the kingdom, to build a community of love, to let something happen that was greater than we were individually.

Just as the Father gives his very self to his children, so must I give my very self to my brothers and sisters.
—The Return of the Prodigal Son

My banker friend helped me see that we must minister to the rich from our own place of wealth—the spiritual wealth we have inherited as brothers and sisters of Jesus Christ. In him "all the jewels of wisdom and knowledge are hidden" (Col. 2:3, NJB). We must have the courage to go to the rich and say, "I love you, and it is not because of your money but because of who you are." We must claim the confidence to go to a wealthy person knowing that he or she is just as poor and in need of love as we are. Can we discover the poor in this person? That is so important because it is precisely in this person's poverty that we discover his or her blessing. Jesus said, "How blessed are you who are poor" (Luke 6:20, NJB). The rich are also poor. So if we ask for money from people who have money, we have to love them deeply. We do not need to worry about the money. Rather, we need to worry about whether, through the invitation we offer them and the relationship we develop with them, they will come closer to God.

Asking

Take away the many fears,
suspicions, and doubts by
which I prevent you from
being my Lord, and give me
the courage and freedom to
appear naked and vulnerable
in the light of your
presence, confident in your
unfathomable mercy.
—*A Cry for Mercy*

ASKING

I F OUR SECURITY IS TOTALLY in God, then we are free to ask for money. Only when we are free from money can we ask freely for others to give it. This is the conversion to which fundraising as ministry calls us. Already we have seen that many people have a hard time asking for money because money is a taboo subject. It is a taboo subject because our own insecurities are connected with it, and so we are not free. We also are not free if we are jealous of the rich and envy their money. And we are not free if we feel anger towards those who have money, saying to ourselves, "I'm not so sure that they made all that money in an honest way." When rich people make us jealous or angry, we reveal that money in some way is still our master and that therefore we are not ready to ask for it.

I am deeply concerned that we do not ask for money out of anger or jealousy, especially when these feelings are well hidden behind polite words and a careful presentation of our request for funds. No matter how polished our approach is, when our asking comes from anger or jealousy we are not giving the person the means to become a brother or sister. Rather, we put the person in a defensive position because he or she realizes that there is some kind of competition going on. The offer to participate in our vision and mission is no longer for the kingdom. It no longer speaks in the name of God, in whom alone our security is secure.

When we truly enjoy God's unlimited generosity, we will be grateful for what our brothers and sisters receive. Jealousy will simply have no place in our hearts.

—Bread for the Journey

Once we are prayerfully committed to placing our whole trust in God and have become clear that we are concerned only for the kingdom; once we have learned to love the rich for who they are rather than what they have; and once we believe that we have something of great value to give them, then we will have no trouble at all in asking someone for a large sum of money. We are free to ask for whatever we need with the confidence that we will get it. That is what the gospel says: "Ask, and it will be given to you;…knock, and the door will be opened to you" (Matt. 7:7, NJB). If for some reason a person says "No," we are free to respond gratefully. We can trust that the Spirit of Christ who is guiding us is also guiding that person. Perhaps her financial resources are more urgently needed elsewhere. Maybe he is not yet ready to make a real commitment. Perhaps we need to listen more deeply to the Spirit so that our asking will be clearer and our vision more attractive. Because we approach potential donors in the Spirit of Christ, when we ask them for money we can do so with an attitude and in an atmosphere of confident freedom. "Christ set us free, so that we should remain free" (Gal. 5:1, NJB).

Asking people for money is giving them the opportunity to put their resources at the disposal of the kingdom. To raise funds is to offer people the chance to invest what they have in the work of God. Whether they have much or little is not as important as the possibility of making their money available to God. When Jesus fed five thousand people with only five loaves of bread and two fish, he was showing us how God's love can multiply the effects of our generosity (see Matt. 14:13-21). God's kingdom is the place of abundance where every generous act overflows its original bounds and becomes part of the unbounded grace of God at work in the world (see 2 Cor. 9:10-15).

A New Communion

Community is the fruit of our
capacity to make the interests
of others more important
than our own.

—*Bread for the Journey*

A NEW COMMUNION

WHEN WE ASK people for money to strengthen or expand the work of the kingdom, we are also inviting them into a new spiritual communion. This is very important. In Paul's letter to the Romans we read: "We are well aware that the whole creation, until this time, has been groaning in labour pains. And not only that: we too, who have the first-fruits of the Spirit, even we are groaning inside ourselves, waiting with eagerness for our bodies to be set free" (Rom. 8:22-23, NJB). This groaning comes from deep within us, and indeed from within all creation. It is the sound of our yearning for communion with God and with one another, a communion that transcends the limitations of time and space.

> *The real danger facing us is to distrust our desire for communion. It is a God-given desire without which our lives lose their vitality and our hearts grow cold.*
> —Here and Now

At the same time, this groaning also expresses God's passionate yearning for communion with us and with all that God created. God desires "that the whole creation itself might be freed from its slavery to cor- ruption and brought into the same glorious freedom as the children of God" (Rom. 8:21, NJB). This is the freedom of true spiritual communion. Asking for money is a way to call people into this communion with us. It is saying, "We want you to get to know us." Gathered together by our common yearning, we begin to know this communion as we move together toward our vision.

We need friends. Friends guide us, care for us, confront us in love, console us in times of pain.
—Bread for the Journey

How does spiritual communion manifest itself concretely? When fundraising as ministry calls us together in communion with God and with one another, it must hold out the real possibility of friendship and community. People have such a need for friendship and for community that fundraising has to be community-building. I wonder how many churches and charitable organizations realize that community is one of the greatest gifts they have to offer. If we ask for money, it means that we offer a new fellowship, a new brotherhood, a new sisterhood, a new way of belonging. We have something to offer—friendship, prayer, peace, love, fidelity, affection, ministry with those in need—and these things are so valuable that people are willing to make their resources available to sustain them. Fundraising must always aim to create new, lasting relationships. I know people whose lives center around the friendship they find in churches, monasteries, service organizations, and intentional Christian communities. These people visit or volunteer, and it is in these settings that they find nurture and support. If these people have money, they will give it; but that is

> *Community is first of all a quality of the heart. It grows from the spiritual knowledge that we are alive not for ourselves but for one another.*
>
> —Bread for the Journey

not the point. When compared with new freedom and new friends in a new communion, the money is the least interesting thing.

Spiritual communion also reveals itself in a new fruitfulness. Here the radical nature of fundraising as ministry becomes clear. In the world, those who raise funds must show potential donors a strategic plan that convinces donors their money will help to increase the productivity and success of the organization. In the new communion, productivity and success may also grow as a result of fundraising. But they are only by-products of a deeper creative energy, the energy of love planted and nurtured in the lives of people in and through our relationship with Jesus. With the right environment and patient care, these seeds can yield a great harvest, "thirty and sixty and a hundredfold" (Mark 4:20). Every time we approach people for money, we must be sure that we are inviting them into this vision of fruitfulness and into a vision that is fruitful. We want them to join us so that together we begin to see what God means when God says, "Be fruitful" (Gen. 1:28).

Finally, I would like to return to the relationship between money and we who seek it through fundraising. Just as the work of building the community of love asks us to be converted in our attitude toward money, so also this same activity invites each of us to greater faithfulness to our personal call, our unique vocation. Our own call must be deepened and strengthened as a result of our fundraising. Sometimes this brings us right to the heart of our struggle with our vocation. During my own fundraising work, people have said to me: "I will give you money if you will take up the challenge to be a better pastor, if you will stop being so busy and be more faithful to your vocation. You run around and talk your head off, but you don't write enough. I know that this is difficult for you—to shut the door and sit behind your desk and not speak to anyone, but I hope that my contribution will support you in your writing." This is part of the fruitfulness of the community of love. By calling us to deeper commitment to our particular ministry, fundraising helps to make visible the kingdom that is already among us.

Prayer and Gratitude

The Spirit reveals that we belong not to a world of success, fame, or power but to God.

—*Bread for the Journey*

PRAYER AND GRATITUDE

HOW DO WE BECOME people whose security base is God and God alone? How can we stand confidently with rich and poor alike on the common ground of God's love? How can we ask for money without pleading, and call people to a new communion without coercing? How can we express not only in our way of speaking but also in our way of being with others the joy, vitality, and promise of our mission and vision? In short, how do we move from perceiving fundraising as an unpleasant but unavoidable activity to recognizing fundraising as a life-giving, hope-filled expression of ministry?

Prayer is the spiritual discipline through which our mind and heart are converted from hostility or suspicion to hospitality toward people who have money. Gratitude is the sign that this conversion is spreading into all aspects of our life. From beginning to end, fundraising as ministry is grounded in prayer and undertaken in gratitude.

Prayer is the radical starting point of fundraising because in prayer we slowly experience a reorientation of all our thoughts and feelings about ourselves and others. To pray is to desire to know more fully the truth that sets us free (see John 8:32). Prayer uncovers the hidden motives and unacknowledged wounds that shape our relationships. Prayer allows us to see ourselves and others as God sees us. Prayer is radical because it uncovers the deepest roots of our identity in God. In prayer we seek God's voice and allow God's word to penetrate our fear and resistance so that we can begin to hear what God wants us to know. And what God wants us to know is that before we think or do or accomplish anything, before we have much money or little money, the deepest truth of our human identity is this: "You are my beloved son. You are my beloved daughter. With you I am well pleased" (see Luke 3:22). When we can claim this truth as true for us, then we also see that it is true for all other people. God is well pleased with us, and so we are free to approach all people, the rich or the poor, in the freedom of God's love. Whether people respond to our fundraising appeal with a "Yes," a "No," or a "Maybe" is less important than the knowledge that we all are gathered as one on the holy ground of God's generous disposition toward us. In prayer, therefore, we learn to trust that God can work fruitfully through us no matter where we are or who we are with.

As our prayer deepens into a constant awareness of God's goodness, the spirit of gratitude grows within us. Gratitude flows from the recognition that who we are and what we have are gifts to be received and shared. Gratitude releases us from the bonds of obligation and prepares us to offer ourselves freely and fully for the work of the kingdom. When we approach fundraising in a spirit of gratitude, we do so knowing that God has already given us what

The more we touch the intimate love of God which creates, sustains, and guides us, the more we recognize the multitude of fruits that come forth from that love.

—Lifesigns

we most need for life in abundance. Therefore our confidence in our mission and vision, and our freedom to love the person to whom we are talking about donating money, do not depend on how that person responds. In this way, gratitude allows us to approach a fundraising meeting without grasping neediness and to leave it without resentment or dejection. Coming and going, we can remain secure in God's love with our hearts set joyfully on the kingdom.

Your
Kingdom
Come

The mystery of ministry is that we have been chosen to make our own limited and very conditional love the gateway for the unlimited and unconditional love of God. Therefore, true ministry must be mutual.

—*In the Name of Jesus*

FUNDRAISING is a very rich and beautiful activity. It is a confident, joyful, and hope-filled expression of ministry. In ministering to each other, each from the riches that he or she possesses, we work together for the full coming of God's kingdom.

Love never ends.

(1 Corinthians 13:8, NJB)

HENRI J. M. NOUWEN'S WORKS CITED

Page 15: *Here and Now* (1994), 83.

Page 17: *Making All Things New* (1981), 57.

Page 19: *¡Gracias!* (1983), 50.

Page 21: *Bread for the Journey* (1997), August 11.

Page 23: *Making All Things New* (1981), 43.

Page 26: *¡Gracias!* (1983), 50.

Page 31: *Here and Now* (1994), 53.

Page 33: *Here and Now* (1994), 40.

Page 34: *Finding My Way Home* (2001), 132.

Page 37: *Reaching Out* (1975), 16.

Page 40: *The Return of the Prodigal Son* (1992), 122.

Page 42: *A Cry for Mercy* (1981), 24.

Page 44: *Bread for the Journey* (1997), July 6.

Page 47: *Bread for the Journey* (1997), January 23.

Page 48: *Here and Now* (1994), 44.

Page 49: *Bread for the Journey* (1997), May 1.

Page 50: *Bread for the Journey* (1997), January 23.

Page 54: *Bread for the Journey* (1997), June 10.

Page 57: *Lifesigns* (1986), 70.

Page 59: *In the Name of Jesus* (1989), 44.

ABOUT HENRI J. M. NOUWEN

Mary Ellen Kronstein

Henri Nouwen and John Mogabgab at Notre Dame in 1978.

Iɴᴛᴇʀɴᴀᴛɪᴏɴᴀʟʟʏ renowned author, respected professor, and beloved pastor, Henri Nouwen wrote over forty books on the spiritual life that have inspired and comforted countless people throughout the world. Since his death in 1996, an ever-increasing number of readers, writers, and researchers are exploring his literary legacy. Henri Nouwen's works have been translated and published in more than twenty-two different languages.

Born in Nijkerk, Holland on January 24, 1932, Nouwen was ordained in 1957. Moved by his desire for a better understanding of human suffering, he went in 1964 to the United States to study in the Religion and Psychiatry Program at the Menninger Clinic. He went on to teach at the University of Notre Dame, the Pastoral Institute in Amsterdam, and the Divinity Schools of both Yale and Harvard, where his classes were among the most popular on campus.

His strong appeal as a teacher and writer had much to do with his passion to integrate all aspects of his life into a lived spirituality. Nouwen was convinced that striving for such integration is an urgent need in our culture. His writing, often autobiographical, gave readers a window into the joys and struggles of their own spiritual quest. The universal character of Nouwen's spiritual vision crossed many boundaries and inspired a wide range of individuals: Wall Street bankers, politicians and professionals, Peruvian peasants, teachers, religious leaders, ministers and care-givers.

Nouwen traveled widely during his lifetime, lecturing on topics such as ministry and caregiving, compassion, peacemaking, suffering, solitude, community, dying and death.

Nouwen was always searching for new images to convey the depth of the good news of the gospel message. For example, Henri met and befriended a group of trapeze artists in a travelling circus. Just prior to his sudden death, he was working on a project to use life in the circus as an image of the spiritual journey. *The Return of the Prodigal Son*, one of his classic works, marries art and spirituality in a contemporary interpretation of the ancient gospel parable.

Henri lived the last ten years of his life with people who have developmental disabilities in a L'Arche community near Toronto, Canada.

Inspired by Henri Nouwen's conviction that one's personal relationship with God is the foundation for all other relationships, the Henri Nouwen Society exists to create opportunities and resources that support people in their desire to grow spiritually.